pet sounds

pet sounds

Stephanie Young

NIGHTBOAT BOOKS
NEW YORK

ISBN: 978-1-937658-94-6

Design and typesetting by HR Hegnauer
Text set in Perpetua

Cataloging-in-publication data is available from the Library of Congress

Nightboat Books
New York
www.nightboat.org

for Clive

If money, according to Augier, "comes into the world with a congenital blood-stain on one cheek," capital comes dripping from head to foot, from every pore, with blood and dirt.

Karl Marx

The family is essentially the institutionalization of our unwaged labor.

Silvia Federici

God only knows what I'd be without you

Brian Wilson

CONGENITAL

I come to you dripping from head to foot
from every pore, you're covered with blood and dirt:
the shape togetherness was taken by

dispossession and constraint

the shape our togetherness took
not exactly our decision
not exactly not

I come to you in the warehouse after work
over lunch I suck you off at a public park
against a backdrop of container ships

you drip from head to foot with bankruptcy
from every pore with debt, I'm covered with
food stamps, worker's comp

faced away from you
dripping with the blood of countless
free applications for student aid

filled out as I instructed
covered with the breath of board
members and executive directors

you enter dripping with nonprofit diversity
and inclusion, I drool onto the cover
its fabric of deans and department chairs

letters of appointment kept and broken
dripping from column to column
from every pore with demographic data

I feel your presence in the joint account
your expenditures and wages
I touch them

AVE I VIA

with reverence
or from the old Norse, kept in check
frightened, restrained, disciplined, fit: *ave*

a formal expression of greeting
birds, small birds

water birds, song birds, wading birds
of paradise, of passage, of prey—
ave migratoria

to be or fare well
now and in the hour of our death

90th Ave, beautifully remodeled
55th Ave, a bungalow ready for your move-in
23rd Ave, built as an ammunition box factory during WWII

the trees that lined them then
the pre-wood trees
in pre-dawn light

I woke in wonder
in night sweats

within a forest dark
within 30 days

on every side a hospital
a hospital complex

the transit village
this our mortal life

more than 600 workers hidden from view
water flowing underground

the RCA TV repair shop
the hot mess house
vanished in a maze

I reawoke to find myself

upon the course of this
upon the road

in the middle of the war against nurses and patient care
halfway along the road we have to go, three cranes

I found that I had strayed into *The Forest*, an American horror
film, *The Forest*, a survival video game, *The Forest*, a plantation

I woke in wonder in literature sunless and dusky—an 1871
    play, a 1903 novel—*The Forest*

I was eating a bagel, hand-rolled
boiled in honey water, baked in a wood fired oven
Montreal-style

either that
or I was eating an oyster

all along the wall
a ladder

I found myself again
climbing

through a night-dark wood, wellbutrin

there were no good choices
and they wouldn't answer my email

I came onto myself
when halfway through

for I did not have a child
for I had moved in a leisurely, casual, or aimless way

confused and with the middle class at strife

wherein men's salaries continue to grow until age 48
reaching $95,000 per year on average

wherein your family obtains coverage under an individual policy '
where, in Jackson county, do they rent to felons

same as it ever was, same as it ever was, same as it ever was
within a shadowed forest

that men pursue
the course of this

our life
so drear

close to the heart of many cafes and shops
153,000 women aged 50 to 64 out of work

letting the days go by
in a park-like setting of trees, gardens, greenbelts, and ponds

where not a vestige of the uncultivated area legally set aside
for hunting by feudal nobility shewed

for the hard fibrous structural tissue was lost,
stems and roots

for a new job get resume and career tips
for a graph of sea level changes

water jets, seaweed wraps, mud baths, and sea-fog inhalation
appeared not anywhere

for I had lost the path
when I lost the straight and narrow waist

when halfway through I found I had vanished
I had been lost to view

alone in a dark wood?
cut your hair

for I had wandered when I had cramps, migraine, bloat,
breast tenderness, mood swings, foggy thinking, losing height

bears, seals, old men, deer, young women, raccoons—
	wandered into town through automatic doors, up to the
	student housing area dripping blood

way off course
way upon

the precipice of this economy
the dark woods wherein a person cries out

I awoke between two families
or subdivisional hierarchies of the same family

I found myself between a browser and a search engine
a CV and a resume
between a facebook page and a facebook group
a large phone and a tablet
pathway financial management and pathway capital partners

the rightful owner and rightful speech
a recession and a depression
the speedup, the slowdown

Clove and Hoof
Hog's Apothecary

your landlord, or anyone acting for your landlord
in tangled ways

I came to in the neighborhood

coveted for its central location, cultural diversity, great climate
the many storied properties have good bones—the breath of
     new life flows through—

two spacious areas, original wood floors
updated Jack and Jill bathroom, walk-in closet

for I had—I knew that I had
dark wood
and never painted over

I'd tear it off
before I let the owner have it

for I knew I had
myself bewildered
the path direct, had failed to keep it

and the people I loved in the woods
where are they now?

where in the United States can you live off the federal
minimum wage of $7.25 an hour?

what was it I even wanted
in the woods, from them—

a little house?
and a great forest, what is that

a prairie, or a swamp
after the money's gone

wholly lost and gone
since missed the right way

into the blue again

I do not even like that song

PET SOUNDS

in the dark I say you are a kitten
and I am a kitten and this makes us
homosexuals. it isn't true

we are mostly straight
old cats. it's the closest I can get.
what is a kitten anyways?

a younger woman who dates older men
something we have done
stout, furry, gray and white moth

totally dependent
the caterpillar of which resembles
highly social animals

I wear a ring, vintage, somebody else's
family heirloom. open metalwork
lets the diamonds shine and look expensive.

when we broke up, some pawn shop
offered only a hundred dollars so I kept it
in a box, as it turns out, for later

even smaller stones sat flush in the band
of my great grandmother's ring
slipped off Heather's finger in some ocean

you wear a silver bracelet

my sister wears it more—rings, children, mostly
around the house. that is a school. six under
the age of ten, lisping, sucking, Avery, Colette,
Chayse, Melania, Beckham, Camden, tending them

teaching them to read. next to the last baby runs
into my legs with the force of a ball sent down a lane
gushing in the tube, *mommy*. I hear his screams
from the parking lot of temporary base housing

happy go next to the last lucky baby boy sounds
short short, long long, pause, go again. something
hundreds of degrees, beetles, protein bars
well past midnight we haul boxes

while her husband sweats in bed. symptoms
by night, development and testing of air force
doctrine by day. until he gets out. maybe he will
maybe he won't. I think I did until these visits

I go to help her house, shaped like the one that raised us
from within its outline observe myself scold Colette
eight, small, crying now, she's tired of doing laundry
why does she have to do all the laundry

Tilikum wears his captivity heavily
twenty six years in a tank
netted off Iceland at the age of two

the matrilines of killer whales
sometimes include one generation
or as many as four

related matrilines travel in a pod
and probably share a past
common maternal ancestor

when Namu, the second orca captured
was brought to Seattle in a floating pen
a pod of 20 followed

the holding tanks the metal holding tanks
and concrete, the tooth raking
and ulcers the boredom

the extreme boredom
the teeth worn down to nubs
and bacterial infection

Dawn Brancheau was blonde and pretty
wore her hair in a ponytail
lay down next to him for a relationship session

after Dine With Shamu he took her
by the hair into his mouth and down
pushed her down with his nose

he wouldn't let go

on the scooter model People 150
your back looks like a boy's
I follow you home from the repair shop

I carry my mother's fear of motorcycles
but not her fear of cancer
my father carried a fear of the heart attack

that killed his father but in the end
a weird form of cancer killed him
and two of his seven siblings

ragged on a country road
in a photo from the childhood
he worked hard to get away from

I like that you are slight
strong jawline big hands

I like the top of your head
the way it smells

the fur that starts on your chest
has gotten thicker with age

you're an otter
a bear

both
neither

some things that really kill me include
you got into the WNBA first
you're all about the squad game not the star

when we fought most recently about working from home
you said three things: open the window sometimes
can you scrape the old man's plate once in a while

I forget the other one

you're ok with me calling the boxer briefs
your panties. when I went to the store for frozen pizza
it felt weird because you do all the shopping.

at SeaWorld you sat with Avery and Colette
and cried or tried not to cry in front of them.
it hurts to be around the way adults are

always putting their hands in the shape of
here is the church, here is the steeple
open the doors, see all the people

we don't own them, so we have no say
in the shape language takes around them

I don't know if we saw Tilikum perform that day

I know he wasn't captured yet in 1972
when Paul Horn played flute with whales
at the Vancouver aquarium
your dad was the sound engineer.

in the 1960s this biologist Roger Payne
first heard whale song on a military recording
meant to capture dynamite explosions. other
sounds kept getting in the way. click, whistle, call

Payne says it is the most complex song of any animal

much was made of whale music
when Greenpeace started, whale intelligence
and emotional sophistication often compared
with humans, and look how that turned out.

Paul Watson is one of those guys
a heroic white dude. you're playing him
this summer in a mash up, that guy and Captain
Ahab, Greenpeace and Moby Dick.

you're always willing to play that guy
that scary damaged guy. in *Troilus and Cressida*
you were sick as Thersites

I still remember it

and that is part of my love too

after the Warriors won last night
we were talking about sports riots generally
you think it's a bad reason to burn a cop car.

I said there's no bad reason to burn a cop car
you said *oh come on*. it was late.
the end of a long day. you had work

then rehearsal. I had bargaining
then plans I couldn't cancel but did
when the cramps came on

I lay on the couch and listened to fireworks
waited for you to come home
watch the game fast forward

through commercials. we already knew
how it turned out, how it was going to.
those are the breaks: the way things happen.

shit. fate. when everything drops out
but the drums. Steph Curry off the dribble.
Steph Curry off the catch. Iguodala

along the perimeter. Iguodala everywhere.
sometimes you catch a break, a stroke of luck
sometimes you wear them down

I didn't watch basketball much before this
I've never actually burned a cop car
you've got me there. I know people have

they will. the breaks are about inevitability
the way things are is the way it goes
what constitutes a break, what makes a break for it

life is short. and life is long. how a thing may contain
the opposite direction of wherever it's headed

a lion that will fly. With his face backward
my favorite line from *Troilus and Cressida*

I think it is about time

that night I dream I inherit property
in another country, an old country
I'm not sure where exactly

my mother's family came from
the small hills of a dark ride
two empty houses on an empty street

I pretend not to care too much about it
symmetrical houses with stuff sticking out
under the cracks. she says don't go in there.

she cries. my mother in a dream

there was never any distance between things
women, wives, land, houses, still
this soft part of the day

this kitten in a world of blood
and dirt, kittens in a world
of shit. our pet. at night

we feed him soup. high calorie
wet food, some water
potassium and methadone

the old man
pumpkin spice
quentin crisp
captain crunch
the chairman
chuckles
mean mr. mustard
mellow yellow
old dirty toenails
old sock
croissockwhich
cutie town
buddy town
baby time

nonreproductive nonsense for a nonhuman companion
I would never call that queer, still

nothing fits

between the first alarm and second
I reach up or you reach down
my mouth hits or your head runs into it
and splits the lip already chapped

I walk around like that all week
with a kind of jelly smeared on top. it takes a while
to heal. don't be that guy, either of them.
don't become that white woman artist.

who was I arguing with back there about cop cars?
I mean I think we mostly agree about that,
you and I, maybe, I'm quick to reconcile difference

a limitation we share
a discomfort with conflict

what happened to your mother happened to you
and your brothers inside the houses that raised us
what else would we be

unmake that problem
so too the sound of you breathing over there
way too loud then again too soft

when you're sleeping I get close and listen
you thought I was dead
sometimes you say what I'm thinking

what force maintains the shapes that maintain us
if not our breathing exactly, the places we get away to
before and after work. just kittens, in a house.

I heard some friends, men, speak beautifully
of all the things they'd miss most
after the, uh, rev

the pop the jazz the blues
all the shapes made possible by slavery
unmake that problem so too its music

couldn't exist. not me, not you and me together
and that's my jam. both things
have to go. those sounds, those guys

I didn't get them. I still don't. I'd miss each other
more than music, myself—can you actually abolish her?

you can try

I say that and Madame George comes into view
sunlight on a dirty windshield
the dry green afternoon

like Shalimar

Van Morrison on repeat. I've only been gone
a little while but your face slips out of range
a photograph taken by phone. I miss it—
I'm driving towards you—I'm lucky—

the song still gets me.
not the Marianne Faithfull version
not *Astral Weeks*, not the love that loves to love
although I have loved that too

I mean Madame George from *TB Sheets*
half as long, unsweet, up against a sick room.
more about falling than what you've lost
what you're going to. The Sweet Inspirations

on backup. Heather gave me that album or
I took it when we broke up. I did that to you
with *Pet Sounds*—the lost objects
of breaking up so often music

what did she tell me about Madame George?
driving home to California, hers not mine yet
probably it is about drugs. I still don't know anything
except how to feel in the car inarticulate

moaning along. we gave the old man pepto
when he got carsick. what were we thinking?
he was just a kitten then for real
we were coming from Spokane
a place so white it felt satanic. she was not.

it was very bad there for her
in ways I cannot fully account for, her best friend
first love dead less than a year before we met

I was running away from home
out of Colorado into the Presbyterian college
where we spent a lot of time in a closet-sized single
dorm room watching *Star Trek*. outside it was the 90s.

when we reached her grandmother's house it was late
or it was early, and jasmine. I stepped on a snail in the half dark.

I wanted this to have that same smell
cool night air up against the bathroom door
the hallway lights begin to dim

that's when you fall
you're in the front room, touching him

those lines don't appear in the Madame George
Lester Bangs wrote about, the dreamy song
Greil Marcus discusses in his book
on Van Morrison. into every love poem

a little Greil Marcus must fall.
he dismisses the version I love most of all
and worse than that The Sweet Inspirations
who he refers to as The Sweet Emotions.

because something is wrong with my brain
because I believe I'm a dumb girl
and men of a certain class know more than me
about music, history, Greil Marcus

must know more than me
I spend a lot of time attempting to figure out
if The Sweet Inspirations ever went
by The Sweet Emotions instead.

they did not. Greil Marcus is wrong.
he is also wrong when he writes

*If one's response to that culture—the culture
as set down by a small number of people
in Mississippi and elsewhere in the American South
from the late 1920s to the early '40s—
is as strong as Van Morrison's plainly was,
how can that culture not be
in the deepest sense one's own?*

Cissy Houston founded The Sweet Inspirations
it's their voices I love in the song. Cissy Houston

with Judy Clay
with Sylvia Shemwell
with Myrna Smith

they released nine albums. sang with
Aretha Franklin, Jimi Hendrix, Helen Reddy
and Elvis, toured with him as backup singers

and warm-up act. in a recording session
on March 28, 1967 they provided backup vocals
for Morrison on his classic hit, Brown Eyed Girl

but in the liner notes for *TB Sheets*
some douche named Michael Ochs
claims the vocals were sung instead

by producer Bert Berns, Jeff Berry,
and Brooks Arthur, the session engineer.

Lauren is writing a poem about justice
including the endless details of injustice
trivia that makes the whole: *when a problem*
touches every point / seeing it should require no art

she says it's like when people thought
the earth was made of turtles or
the earth was flat and rested on a turtle's back
resting on top of another, turtles
all the way down. this story, obvious and old

complicated and not. The Sweet Inspirations version
of Madame George ends with all the little boys
coming around with gold cigarette lighters
in their pocket. something got at her expense
as they walk away from her—so cool.

the story goes that Morrison got screwed over
by the producer on those sessions.

I like the piece about his dad's record collection
best in Ulster, acquired in Detroit, and at least

he says *if it weren't for guys like Ray
and Solomon, I wouldn't be where I am today.*

Twenty Feet From Stardom received nearly
universal positive reviews. everybody knows.
everything I love is born of brutal contact.

if Madame George is, like Bangs said
and Morrison denied, a lovelorn drag queen

why should that be the saddest thing
to write a sad song about? and if she is

the wife of Yeats, his medium and muse?
more or less sad? Morrison said it's whatever
you want it to be. a swiss cheese sandwich.

that sounds a lot like a woman
or something a woman would make for him

Bangs wrote *when the singer hurts him*
we do too. I don't know, Madame George seems
incredibly hot to me. in charge of the room.
it makes more sense when she says
be cool be cool I think that it's the cops
not *lord have mercy* in *Astral Weeks*
she's helpless. acted upon. another reason
The Sweet Inspirations version, ok
I just want to keep saying that
until it's a thing, is vastly superior

she does not throw her hands up, she seems to me
that one, like you, with me, in the room
where something like knowledge comes into focus

gets undone

Madame George, 21 or 22
how was it I could stand the crowds
at Grateful Dead shows, 25

our first fight at Office Depot
I got upset you selected for me.
gel pens and fluorescent post-its

our first workplace theft.
you were accounts payable
I was accounts receivable. our first joke.

we both worked downstairs
and there was an upstairs. was there ever.
you were 12 years older and married to Bonnie

I was with Heather, it felt safe
it didn't cross my mind
when I finally came out to my family

badly, she was too angry to help.
I talked to you instead. *sitting on a sofa
playing games of chance.*

by the time we slept together
it felt perverse, fucking a man

a few weeks ago someone gave us free tickets
to the Dead reunion tour. it's a long time since
steal your face on the back of my raincoat, hers
on the smoking deck with you at work
when it still rained

when we get to the stadium
there's no parking lot no tents no drums
a lot of men inside
a festival of aggressive dancing in a feminine way
or a weird idea of feminine softness
alongside the worst sort of collecting
and collector behavior. man buns.
it's our first show together.

I lick stuff from the palm of your hand.
nostalgia fever

shouting JERRY from the floor or WE'RE READY
the time it rained in Vegas, lightning
her hand holding mine so I wouldn't get lost

I cultivated a style of not knowing the names of any songs
called everything you could not dance to space mountain.
she was the expert. played collectors off one another

men who would have ripped us off: two girls
in our dorm room kind of way. those guys came to the house
once. she beat them back with devil sticks

made from electrical tape and strips of leather
more often used for juggling, things she made and sold
on tour. I was the femme in this situation

which felt like bait. I hated getting high until that summer
Modesto or Mt. Hood where I stayed in the tent keeping my books
dry by day, vomiting into my boots by night. passed out

after selling plasma. blew my nose into her favorite hat
during a fight, the Mao hat her grandmother brought back
from China, her white grandmother who travelled the world

and raised her, who had money her father didn't want her to have.
I had no experience of going back and forth
between having a lot of money then none.

I only knew how to get a job.
a low paying job.
she wanted us to have a vision.

at the stadium our seats are really high
two flags fly along the perimeter
one national, one rainbow

the supreme court decision came down
June 26th, same day same anniversary
we shared then broke it, yours with Bonnie

mine with Heather. I message *hi*
guess where I am congratulations.
she married Caitlin earlier this summer

they have that way of looking in photographs
the right amount alike, of corresponding
like Catherine and Elliot and Lindsey and Steve

there is an excellent image of her
giving someone the finger. that thing
she whispered in your ear

when she showed up at the office
when it was going down
stay away from my lady, white boy

the poem is long, like life
soupy, thick with it
I go away with not men to the country

you are in rehearsal again
a play about solitary confinement
you are the white man in this play

a swastika will be painted on your chest
and neck every night before the show
I wonder will an outline remain

when you wash it off, what will it be like
for the next six weeks

you are frustrated that the script
depicts the white man as having moved
beyond his racism, that his speech

after years of silence instigates the hunger strike
at Pelican Bay, a multiracial coalition, a play of uplift
sort of. you are frustrated with many things

not depicted there that might have made it more
like life, uncomfortable, or more clear
how those men arrived together

at the point of striking. it can't have been easy.
we argue over this. but a script is not a play
and I think that tattoo will do a lot of work

language can't. your character's unabashed
sexism though
remains

in dialogue

I'm scared of everything
like a dog, it's all exciting

putting on mascara
waiting for the tree people

Yedda told us their name
but not what they do, she saw my face

and stopped. when I was little
I thought closed for the season

was a horror film. we agree
the country scares us more

country cops, 400 acres
when the road narrows

then the pavement runs out
narrows again, a bridge, a gate

a padlock, a combination
scares me most

when it opens onto a meadow
a house in a clearing

anything I have
once I understand
I have it

Prageeta Sharma is writing about
Dale Edwin Sherrard, 1961-2015

Prageeta's husband
Dale died last year
he was 53 years old

his memoir is called *When You Could Smoke on Airplanes*

I watch the videos as Prageeta posts them
read her Cassavetes poem, the one Dale loved

about teaching about race
in Montana, and men

I don't know Prageeta
I didn't know Dale

you were born in 1961, the same as Dale
Prageeta was born in 1972, a few years before me

she is writing through it, in public
says closure happens for her through talking

or *closure isn't closure but openings*

I thought for a long time
A Woman is Talking to Death
referred to a woman talking a lot
as in talking you to death
something I do all the time
open one sentence after another
close some later get annoyed
when you seem distracted

in the classroom too, if it were more mixed
if I didn't teach at a mostly women's college I bet
I'd be taken less seriously the way I've let myself
go, powerpoint slide with too many boxes
too many arrows between them
so that everything seems to be connected
COINTELPRO, Redstockings, *Deep Throat*

maybe I mixed up Judy Grahn with Pat Parker

I'm beginning to
wonder if
the tactics
of this revolution
    is to
talk the enemy to death

Parker means *the enemy*
she means *this revolution* too

Judy Grahn means death
who keeps us from / our lovers
the black man she leaves on the bridge
the women she didn't hold didn't kiss
the one with a knife she didn't want
to sleep with—too fat too old too ugly—

she's writing this in 1974
this woman is a lesbian be careful
this lesbian, separate from men

so it's a big deal when she leaves him
on the bridge when she writes
as I have left so many of my lovers
that he should be counted among them
in 1974, Judy Grahn knows who the enemy is

six big policemen

who her lovers are
and the wind

could blow them all over the edge

full looking moon waning gibbous
Jupiter now nearly as bright as it will be
all year, year of the monkey

the night Joanie passes
when I get home from work
four cop cars one ambulance

police move through the house in uniform
Michael on the sidewalk a little high a little drunk
hasn't slept for days asking *what, do they think*

I killed her? we stand in a semi circle and touch.
they shouldn't be here, why are they still here
the ambulance is gone, Joanie is gone

someone says the coroner is coming
you can see how this situation could go wrong
Michael says she opened her eyes and kissed him

just before she left they were talking, he looked up
removed her dentures so she wouldn't gag

catches himself, she wasn't going to gag

anyways he took them out

you stay up with him that night
a bottle of bourbon from Bernadette's reading
between our houses in the driveway
listen to your voices as I fall asleep thinking
that little bottle is just the right size

I don't know how old Joanie was
or Michael is, older than him but not by much

they hung out in high school
in the neighborhood
on the block

his parents bought the house next door
mid 1960 something, one of the first black families
on the street. all the white ones flew away

mostly, not Joanie's. I don't know why. Clive
interrupts—if you were on the block
back then you were poor. then came the 80s

glass pipes, Mosswood Park, now proximity
drives up the price. Clive coughs. Michael coughs.

it wasn't until he introduced me to someone else
as Jennifer that I corrected him and hurt his feelings

I didn't say anything before because I didn't want to
hurt his feelings or make either of us uncomfortable

plus tbh it amused me

Joanie, Jennifer, Stephanie
white girls
white girl names

my father was only 63, nine years older than you now
his father was only 50, four years younger
and yours was only 53, your age last year

denial, repression, acting out
projection, displacement, dissociation

premature elegy

riding around on a blow up dolphin
in the pool with my friends
you're not here but it feels like you are
extruding all these pieces in the water

I remember how pretty Bonnie was
dancing in a long skirt, how she squirted breast milk
over the van, the time she was superwoman
for Halloween even though I was never there

she careened through the photo of you and Mark
last weekend I caught it. your ex-wife, your brother, your
family. sometimes it's still a little weird. sometimes I forget
we're not going to have kids. these aren't exactly

sonnets. I tried, but they didn't turn.

you didn't go to college or grow up with money
but in a suit you pass for a businessman
walking up Durant to rehearsal some Cal students
drove by in a truck. *fuck you faggot suck my dick.*

in a photograph on the boat your family took
from Scotland to Vancouver, you and your brothers
wear red wellies and pajamas. three small santas
some kind of pageant. after they moved everyone to California

you found your parents in bed new years day morning
with friends and the head of a suckling pig
which is to say your dad made some money in the 70s
but spent it all on clothes and Le Central

where he barely touched the food. smoked
endless cigarettes, drank endless brandies.

when your boss sexually harassed you
nobody including us knew what to do

when a rich white married gay guy with a lot of power
harasses a not rich white married bisexual guy
with a medium amount of power

the co-pay for an appointment I pushed you to
make this morning came to $360 after all the tests
because nonprofit insurance sucks so bad

you said you're taking yourself out to lunch
you're looking up the thing it could be
the thing you asked me please not to look up

I'm writing this in my office at work
because you're home sick. I knew
if I worked there I'd take care of you instead.

maybe you also meet your own needs
by meeting the needs of others. I think so.

that I do may or may not mean anything
about how far we haven't come. I am not
every woman. every woman is not in me.

every paper bag looks like the cat

from the corner of my eye
every F150 is white, I see you everywhere
in the truck we named T&A

basic shittiness of private language
in the private household
anything is permitted

the biggie smalls of your back
baby townes van zandt
the dirty version of every song

but when you sing *I saw mommy kissing
santa's balls* the joke always seems to be
on santa, christmas, family at all

vertiginous shaded figures

I have a way of watching *Grey's Anatomy*
from behind my hand to block the lower half
red bags of liquid, open cavities

in the constellation aquarius there is a star called binka
you registered my private name with money
everybody knows you cannot own a star

contained within the heart of a gem
I sit on the kitchen table kicking my legs

talking, honestly, nonsense
in the house who were we even

sometimes you said things out loud
things you couldn't say at work

sometimes I stopped you
sometimes I didn't

you're a little too good at speaking on my behalf
at the holiday dinner I sit between you
my mother, her husband, reproduction
everywhere and wonder why we pass
or do we pass? for what? lumpen, wifeish
I know when they ask *now tell us*
what's been going on at work they can't listen.
only men have jobs. why do I care. even though
we agreed on this tactic in the car on the way there
or after we fucked in the bed my sister grew up in
next door to a brass headboard I leaned against
as a child and had bad dreams about touching myself
or being touched as I came, it still feels horrible.

I love to talk
I really love to talk

I like to appear as a person

you have never stolen money from
or raped me, never fucked my classmates
called me cheap or screamed all night
and cried because I made a joke about chapstick
at a party when I was nervous you never said
I was a slut for flirting or called me prude
because I didn't want to get you off over email
because I already had enough work to do
and that guy wanted me to do it for free

you forgave me for going back to him
a second and third time even though
he never made me come, not once

in retrospect I did think odd things
about your gender and care, like it would be
less work and you would purchase
all the furniture. we sank into the drag of that
for years, its credit card debt

after fifteen years I finally got used to you
working days and nights and weekends
rehearsal every day except Friday for a month
followed by Thursday, Friday, Saturday, Sunday
evening shows for another month. when it ends
you miss the temporary backstage family
or you're relieved, let down, we're tired

it starts over. I'd wait up for you every night.
we never got enough sleep. it's ok I told myself
I liked this schedule. it allowed me time to write
which is true but also a defense against feeling
lonely. when I did you weren't always patient

I think you felt bad, or if you paused
my feelings might have stopped you.

then it shifted

I don't love the way you feel you'll never work again
when you're not working on a play. your mom
could have had a music career if it wasn't for you
your brothers, your dad, the war, the hospital
so you couldn't have one either. theater was a substitute.
I know you think that. I'm not sure it's true.
I tell you to say yes when casting directors call
I do a lot of work to convince you

when I'm gone for a day or a week for a panel or conference
or reading, you get lonely, visibly lonely, and have no problem
being vocal about it like the cat who meows and meows
when I'm gone and I know is very hard to live with

I can't figure out how much I've let this stop me

you took me to emergency
when I was projectile vomiting
and thought it was a heart attack

you thought I was nuts until I explained
symptoms show up differently in women
can include exhaustion and a sense of doom

also it runs in my family

now we have a ziplock bag
anti-nausea pills that dissolve
under the tongue

I am feeling pretty smart

I remember someone smarter than me
said if you are not thinking about HIV meds
how to get them after the revolution
then you are missing something about the revolution

when you are feeling little like today
hold out your arms or point to the top of your head
it's disconcerting

you rarely allow yourself to cry
and are good at stopping once you've started
in the car with Brokedown Palace

do you want lotion, a kiss, what

I can't tell what's going on there
in the song, I mean

you remind me how it ends
lovers come and go

yes but did his one true love leave? is she dead?
or with him, and all the others

left, or died
flown away

it feels very true
to the feeling

regardless
either way

going to leave this brokedown palace
on my hands and my knees

will I always feel this way?

nostalgia washes back through Ripple
driving back down the road we drove up from the forest
when you fell in mud and jammed your wrist

when Chayse screams and cries because Melania is staring at him
she probably is, he's 18 months older, a lot
my sister laughs it's like getting angry at a teddy bear

how can people hate the Grateful Dead

it was that season, the anniversary of his death
you were in the plaid shirt he wore on weekends
navy wool my dad wore in the garage

a paddle with holes and two yardsticks hung by the door

I put it on and drank a beer
it's gotten so soft

it's a hand me down
the thoughts are broken

for every Ripple
China Doll
Fare Thee Well

there is Bob singing *what is a man*
deep down inside

Jerry singing *we can share the women*
we can share the wine

or myself, at the top of my lungs, with everyone else

Tennessee Tennessee
there ain't no place I'd rather be

for every you
there is another kind of him

for every part of you that isn't
a part that is

a long line of trains
run through those songs

sound of its whistle in Tennessee Jed
he can't go back, he's compelled to
rich man stepped on his head

written by Robert Hunter in Barcelona
topped up on vino tinto
strolling through the european city

I wish that I could want to be
a headlight on a northbound train
or high on cocaine
I wish I'd rather be in some dark hollow

women with their hair hanging down
they can never be easy

women and liquor
women and money

pretty brown-eyed loving machines

I sang the chorus with you on ukulele
that's right the women are smarter
in the living room until I ran out of breath
the women are smarter that's right
each side of the coin the same

they are gone
they are waiting

they lay their head down in the roses

like men
women terrify me

I never know what form
their misogyny will take

something like a bird within them sings

when you were small
you were eldest
and held responsible

when your dad was on the road
if your mom was upset
when he came home

she was always upset
often alone in the house
with three small children

she put whiskey in your milk
whiskey in your tea

when you were teething
when you cried

if the module had been deeper
or not made of steel
if the tank had been wider

if the orca show hadn't been performed
every hour on the hour eight times a day
seven days a week

if they were not left in the module
fourteen hours every night, if they could have
moved without cuts and scratches

if the older females hadn't been
sorting out the pecking order
if Tilikum wasn't small and male

trainers say he was their favorite
the one they really liked to work with
youthful, energetic, eager to learn

I like to sing along low, then high

I'm going away
I'm leaving today
going but I ain't coming back

it isn't true
when I long it's for return

when I came out my dad said
I was going to hell. he didn't want
to speak with me again

when I got together with you
I wonder if I was trying to get back
together with him, at first

it worked like that
you were a man

quickly not the one
he wanted

divorced, vasectomy

growing up in that house my mother ruled
from the bottom at least its spending

he fell asleep on the couch after work
or on top of the covers in BVDs

we laughed over him from the hallway
not without affection

when he had walking pneumonia in winter
I beat on his back with my fists when it burned
in summer and peeled I picked skin from it

when we all went to England
the year before his diagnosis
my sister's husband was stationed there

in the country in its suburb
my mother sent me with him on a day trip
to London, I felt, in her place

but he was interested in me as a son
I wanted him to be

you're wearing a suit opening night
at the new UC theater, classically

scratchy wool, on the advisory board
glad I didn't wear heels and dance

you hold the wall
with your chin cast like a man

we go back the next night
in civilian cords and t shirt, in disguise

I say honey
let your femme flag fly

hold the wall for you
cast my chin

straight mostly white women are coming out
this week on the internet
with their desire for all the genders

after a man killed 50 people
in a dance club queer people
mostly brown and black people

in a church a kind of church

I shift uncomfortably in my chair

discourse within myself
if everyone is queer would nobody get hurt?

if Lenny Bruce was right if you empty out the word
or fill it up, if it didn't matter who used it
if fighting relatives in red states—*defriend me now*

if you don't like it—did anything stopped any kid
in any skirt from getting lit on fire any brown or black
person in a church a kind of church

if people could just identify queerness
with mostly straight white women
their desire for all the genders

what happened to Stacy, Amanda
Oscar, Rodolfo, Antonio, Darryl
Angel, Juan, Luis, Cory, Tevin
Deonka, Simon, Leroy, Mercedez
Peter, Juan, Paul, Frank, Miguel
Javier, Jason, Eddie, Anthony
Christopher, Alejandro, Brenda
Gilberto, Kimberly, Akyra
Luis, Geraldo, Eric, Joel
Jean, Enrique, Jean, Xavier
Christopher, Yilmary, Edward
Shane, Martin, Jonathan, Juan
Luis, Franky, Luis and Jerald

was never the same as what
happened to you or me

faggot, dyke

what didn't kill us
didn't kill us

I call you my husband when the PG&E
rate guy comes around pounding on our door
it's true, the bill is in your name

I call you my person mostly
I said partner for a while

it felt wrong
it doesn't matter

if I could disinvest us of the categories
what's left? two cat ladies
two men and a baby who is a cat
older than us both combined
like Benjamin Button I hold him
to my chest he scrapes
his chin on the side of my breast
I put him down abruptly

he will die before us
the truck will go before you
and you probably before me
whose blue book value so declined
I will have become a cat lady
without a pet

what passed for a series of choices in my lifetime

there's the time a key broke off in my hand
stranded at the lake

I walked back towards you slowly
a bad thing happened

there's your brother walking in on you and Rick
and telling everyone

at Sunday dinner a friend of the family announced
ask Clive, isn't he the gay now?

there's your father, then mine
there's Rick

gone not long before we met
I was never there but it feels like I was

methamphetamine, the Santa Cruz mountains
kiddie pools

there's his nickname for you, *clittie*
and a lodge rented by the city for special events

our wedding, your brother's, the memorial
a bench engraved with my father's name at Denver Seminary

where his ashes blew back in my face
like a romantic comedy

what was it we even wanted
in the woods, from them—

a little house?

your mom lives in the cottage behind Bonnie
Randy stays with Bonnie most of the time

we take care of your mom some of the time
she takes care of Mark by letting him care for her

most of the time, the hardest parts
getting in and out of the shower

Randy and Mark don't speak

Michael visits Joanie's sister in the nursing home
calls his new roommate partner, it sounds like business partner

we transfer money to your mom's account
for rent she pays Bonnie

the US census would say, I think, that Michael and his roommate
form a household, all the members living in a given housing unit

I'm not sure if the US census would say that Bonnie and Randy
and your mom and Mark form a household, or a family household

The US census says you and I are a family household with two
members related by birth, marriage, or adoption, a married
couple without own children, any age—Heather and Caitlin a
family household with three members, a married couple with
own children under three years—my sister and her husband
a family household with seven or more members, a married
couple with own children more than one age group, some under
six years, some 6-11

stuffed full
it still doesn't explode

despite every shape that crashes there
upon the category

the way water tends to run around all obstacles

or the way large wave pools channel excess water through a
return canal

where it can be used to generate another wave

I almost steal a stalk of what isn't yarrow

the sage with purple flowers
I stole outside Brandon's old apartment
is doing pretty well, making roots

everybody knows you cannot own a plant

our labor made the patio and garden
purchased wages to obtain this umbrella
casting shade over a green plastic table
I haggled down to fourteen dollars

what was in your wallet
what we found on the street

patio furniture from the set
after that play was over, the one about
math, dusted with grey spray paint
to look authentic

it looks authentic

we don't own the house
or the yard or the shed
we covered in a tarp

I'm learning to tell the difference

ACKNOWLEDGMENTS

"AVE | VIA" was inspired by and departs from Caroline Bergvall's poem *Via*.

Thanks to the editors of *About a Bicycle*, *Cordite Poetry Review*, *P Queue*, and *Lana Turner Journal* where some of these poems first appeared. Thanks, also, to curators at the Berkeley Art Museum who included a poem from *Pet Sounds* in the *Way Bay* postcard series.

I am indebted to friends who read early versions of, commented on, and supported this work in ways that made it possible to write. Thank you to Lindsey Boldt, Brandon Brown, Samantha Giles, Claire Grossman, Angela Hume, Lauren Levin, Trisha Low, Pam Martin, Catherine Meng, Yedda Morrison, Christian Nagler, Ron Palmer, Jocelyn Saidenberg, Eric Sneathen, Juliana Spahr, Syd Staiti, Alli Warren, and Chet Wiener.

STEPHANIE YOUNG lives and works in Oakland. Her books of poetry and prose include *It's No Good Everything's Bad*, *Ursula or University*, *Picture Palace*, and *Telling the Future Off*. She edited the anthology *Bay Poetics*, and with Juliana Spahr, *A Megaphone: Some Enactments, Some Numbers, and Some Essays about the Continued Usefulness of Crotchless-pants-and-a-machine-gun Feminism*. Young is a member of the Krupskaya editorial collective.

NIGHTBOAT BOOKS

Nightboat Books, a nonprofit organization, seeks to develop audiences for writers whose work resists convention and transcends boundaries. We publish books rich with poignancy, intelligence, and risk. Please visit nightboat.org to learn about our titles and how you can support our future publications.

The following individuals have supported the publication of this book. We thank them for their generosity and commitment to the mission of Nightboat Books:

Kazim Ali
Anonymous
Jean C. Ballantyne
Photios Giovanis
Amanda Greenberger
Anne Marie Macari
Elizabeth Motika
Benjamin Taylor
Jerrie Whitfield & Richard Motika

Nightboat Books gratefully acknowledges support from the Topanga Fund, which is dedicated to promoting the arts and literature of California.